THE STORY OF THE OLYMPIC GAMES

WELBECK

Published in 2020 by Welbeck

An Imprint of Welbeck Non-Fiction Limited, part of Welbeck Publishing Group
20 Mortimer Street, London W1T 3JW

Design © Welbeck Non-Fiction Limited, part of Welbeck Publishing Group
First published by Carlton Books Limited in 2008

Designed by: Rockjaw Creative

Executive Editor: Suhel Ahmed

Design Manager: Matt Drew

A CIP catalogue record for this book is available from the British Library

ISBN 978-1-78312-551-7

Printed in Dubai

10 9 8 7 6 5 4 3 2 1

PICTURE CREDITS

The publishers would like to thank the following sources for their kind
permission to reproduce the pictures in this book.

All photographs are the copyright of the OLYMPIC MUSEUM and
INTERNATIONAL OLYMPIC COMMITTEE with the exception of the following:

GETTY IMAGES: 45B; /AFP: 31L, 49TR, 55L, 59BL, 61L; /The Asahi Shimbun: 51BL; /Simon Bruty:
78B; /Vince Caligiuri/The Age/Fairfax Media: 75L; /Central Press: 26BR, 39BR, 49BL; /Jerry Cooke/
Sports Illustrated: 59TL; /A R Coster: 30TR; /Tony Duffy: 66L; /Julian Finney: 83BL; /Stu Forster:
87TR; /Gamma-Rapho: 77L; /Alexander Hassenstein/Bongarts: 75TR; /Scott Heavey: 87L; /Tommy
Hindley/Professional Sport/Popperfoto: 81BR; /Hulton Archive: 6, 67L; /Ishi/Keystone/Hulton
Archive: 51T; /Jed Jacobsohn: 85BL; /Keystone: 48TR, 56C; /Richard Mackson/Sports Illustrated:
68BR; /Clive Mason: 90BR; /Richard Meek /Sports Illustrated: 45TR; /Manny Millan/Sports
Illustrated: 65L; /Pascal Pavani/AFP: 71R; /Hannah Peters: 90L; /Photo12/UIG: 35TL; /Popperfoto:
11BL, 47TL; /Mike Powell: 69L, 71TR; /Michael Regan: 4-5; /Rolls Press/Popperfoto: 53TL, 60BR; /
Vladimir Rys/Bongarts: 80-81; /Bob Thomas Sports Photography: 81TR; /Topical Press Agency:
17BR; /David Turnley/Corbis/VCG: 64BR; /ullstein bild: 25R

MARY EVANS: /Illustrated London News Ltd: 29L

PA IMAGES: /Empics Sport: 31BR, 36B; /Topham Picturepoint: 50B

SHUTTERSTOCK: /AP: 12BR, 53BL, 54BR

Every effort has been made to acknowledge correctly and contact the source
and/or copyright holder of each picture, any unintentional errors or omissions
will be corrected in future editions of this book.

CONTENTS

INTRODUCTION

The Olympic Games is the world's biggest sporting festival. It has more competitors, more spectators and is watched by more people around the world than any other sporting event.

For more than a century, the cities around the world have sought to host the event, and men and women everywhere have dedicated their lives to training for it. Some have given perfect medal-winning performances, and others have felt despair when their hard work hasn't led them to victory. All of them have played a part in creating the magic of the Olympic Games, and inspiring generations of people to do something amazing.

The modern Olympic Games is adapted from the Greek sporting festival of the ancient Olympic Games. The idea to create a modern festival was dreamt up by a French man named Pierre de Coubertin in 1892. He thought that sports should be used to educate people. This idea is still at the heart of the Olympic Games today.

Put together with help from The Olympic Museum and the International Olympic Committee, this book is a journey through the history of the modern Olympic Games, from the first simple celebration in Athens in 1896 to the stunning spectacle it is today.

The Opening Ceremony of the 2012 Olympic Games in London.

OLYMPIC ORIGINS

The ancient Olympic Games were held more than 3,000 years ago, in ancient Olympia in Greece. When archeologists discovered the site of these Games in 1766, it sparked people's imaginations. Ancient history was set to become modern history.

Ancient history

The ancient Olympic Games were held every four years in honour of the Greek god Zeus. The programme of events included religious ceremonies as well as sporting competitions. Messengers called *spondophori* travelled around Greece spreading the word about the Games and calling for athletes and spectators to come to Olympia.

This engraved picture shows athletes and spectators at ancient Olympia.

Early sports

Only one sporting competition featured in the earliest-known edition of the ancient Olympic Games in 776 BC. It was a sprint, which was the length of the stadium, called a *stade*. Later, more competitions appeared. The *diaulos* was a sprint of double the length of the stadium. The pentathlon, boxing, wrestling, chariot races, a race in armour and the *pankration* were also added to the programme.

This vase shows a *quadriga*, a four-horse chariot, in ancient Greece.

Stars of Olympia

Leonadis of Rhodes won three running events at each of the Games from 164 to 152 BC. Phanas of Pellene was the first man to win three events at a single Games in 514 BC. Although Belestiche could not compete in the chariot race in 268 BC, as the chariot owner, she was credited with the win.

To protect their naked bodies athletes rubbed oil and sand into their skin. This oil flask would have been worn on an athlete's wrist.

Pierre de Coubertin's idea

Inspired by the ancient Olympic Games, in 1892 Pierre de Coubertin thought that a modern version of the ancient sports festival could be a great way to celebrate sporting achievements. In 1894 he told people about his idea, and two years later his dream became a reality with the first edition of the modern Olympic Games in Athens.

Pierre de Coubertin was passionate about sports and his idea for the modern Olympic Games.

1896
ATHENS

Known as the I Olympiad, the first modern Olympic Games might have had athletes from only 14 countries taking part, but the people of Greece were so enthusiastic about the event that it proved a huge success.

GAMES STATS

Opening date:
6 April 1896

Closing date:
15 April 1896

Country of host city:
Greece (GRE)

Nations: 14

Events: 43

The people's Games

Once the honour of hosting the first celebration of the modern Olympic Games was given to the Greek capital city, it was the people of Athens who helped make the project happen. They raised more than 332,756 Greek drachma for the event. A wealthy Greek businessman, George Averoff, paid the 920,000 drachma that was needed to restore the ancient Panathenaic Stadium.

This was one of 12 Greek stamps issued to raise funds for the I Olympiad.

The reconstructed Panathenaic Stadium was built from marble and seated 40,000 people for the 1896 Opening Ceremony.

FAST **FACT**

The swimming events in I Olympiad were held at sea. Competitors were taken out in boats and left in the water to swim back to shore!

Impressive Americans

Thirteen American students travelled for three weeks to reach Athens for the Games. Despite referring to the wrong calendar and arriving later than planned, many triumphed in the athletics events. Notably, James Connolly became the first modern Olympic champion when he won the triple jump. Another American, Thomas Burke, won the 100 metres final.

Marathon pride

A crowd of 100,000 people gathered in and around the stadium to watch the marathon, cheering on the 12 Greek runners among the 17 athletes in the race. They weren't disappointed – a Greek competitor, Spiridon Louis, won the event. The crowd cheered "Hellene! Hellene!" (meaning "Greek! Greek!") as Louis raced to the finish line.

Spiridon Louis wins the 1896 marathon, cheered on by huge crowds.

Winners' prizes

All first-place winners in I Olympiad won a silver medal, a crown of olive leaves and a diploma that featured the Greek goddess Nike and the ruins of the ancient Parthenon. Second-place winners received a copper medal, a laurel crown and a diploma.

The first-place silver medal, featuring the Greek god Zeus and winged Victory (a Greek goddess), and the prize diploma.

ΔΙΕΘΝΕΙΣ ΟΛΥΜΠΙΑΚΟΙ ΑΓΩΝ
ΑΠΟΝΕΜΕΤΑΙ ΤΟ ΔΙΠΛΩΜΑ ΤΟΥΤΟ
ΝΙΚΗΣΑΝΤΙ ΕΝ ΤΩ, ΑΓΩΝΙΣΜΑΤΙ
Ο ΠΡΟΕΔΡΟΣ.
Ο ΓΕΝ. ΓΡΑΜΜΑΤΕΥΣ.

1900 PARIS

Paris became the second city to host the modern Olympic Games in 1900. These Games were sometimes overshadowed by another event – the Paris World's Fair – but that didn't stop the athletes from putting on an amazing show and creating Olympic history.

GAMES STATS

Opening date:
14 May 1900

Closing date:
28 October 1900

Country of host city:
France (FRA)

Nations: 24
Events: 95

Entry tickets for the 1900 Paris World's Fair, of which the Games were a part.

A cup showing the Eiffel Tower and six monuments of the Paris World's Fair.

FAST FACT

Unlike later Olympic Games, teams of the 1900 celebration were often made up of individuals from more than one country!

Joint spectacle

Unlike the Games of the I Olympiad, this edition of the Games was part of a World's Fair, also called the Universal Exposition. Tickets, medals and souvenirs often featured the French words "Exposition Universelle" instead of "Olympic". As a result, it was sometimes difficult to tell which programmes were part of the Games and which belonged to the fair. Some spectators and athletes didn't even realise it was the Olympic Games that they were watching or taking part in!

Female Olympians

Women took part in the Olympic Games for the first time in Paris 1900. The legends of some of the 22 female competitors live on to this day. Britain's Charlotte Cooper took home two gold medals and became the first Olympic tennis champion. USA's Margaret Abbott competed against her mother, Mary, among others, in a golf tournament to become the first American woman to win an Olympic gold medal.

A poster created by Jean de Paleologu for the fencing competitions. Although it shows a woman, no females took part in the fencing events.

Short-lived sports

The Games in 1900 featured some sports that were introduced to the Olympic programme for the first time, then quickly disappeared before returning in later Games. Polo and even a tug-of-war competition were part of these Games. A combined team from Sweden and Denmark won the tug-of-war gold medal.

American Charles Sands won the golf competition in Paris. After 1904 golf was no longer an Olympic sport until it was reintroduced at the 2016 Olympic Games.

Athletic advertising

Olympic champions were used to advertise products for the first time in 1900. New Yorker John Flanagan won the hammer-throw competition at the Games in Paris. His win was celebrated as part of a series of cards that were used to advertise tobacco.

The USA's John Flanagan won the first of his hammer titles in Paris. His victory was celebrated on a cigarette card issued by Hassan.

THE STARS OF
ATHENS 1896

All but 90 of the 241 competitors in the I Olympiad were Greek, and only 13 other nationalities took part. The people of Athens were overjoyed to cheer a fellow Greek to victory in the marathon, a new event that was inspired by the Greek legend of Pheidippides.

🇬🇷 Spiridon Louis

When this 24 year old from a village outside Athens won the first Olympic marathon, he made Greek history and even became part of the language. The expression "egine Louis" in Greek came to mean "run quickly" after his victory. The Greek people showered him with gifts but he would only accept a horse and cart from the King to help him in his job – transporting fresh water twice a day from his village to Athens.

🇺🇸 James Connolly

James Connolly was the American champion in the triple jump before he travelled to Athens in 1896. A student at Harvard University, he was refused permission to leave his studies and compete in the Olympic Games so he dropped out of his course. He won the triple jump, came joint second in the high jump and took third place in the long jump.

THE STARS OF
PARIS 1900

Athletes at the Games in Paris put on a great show, demonstrating their sporting abilities and creating Olympic history. Britain's Charlotte Cooper triumphed in two tennis tournaments. Meanwhile, in the men's track-and-field events, among the standout winners was US jumper Ray Ewry.

Ray Ewry

American Ray Ewry was an unlikely contender for Olympic glory. He contracted polio as a child and was in a wheelchair. Once he could walk again, he strengthened his legs by jumping. Nicknamed the "human frog", he became brilliant at the standing jump – the long, the high and the triple – winning all three events at the Games in both 1900 and 1904, as well as the standing high jump and the standing long jump in London in 1908.

Charlotte Cooper

Nicknamed "Chattie", Charlotte Cooper was a Londoner who played tennis wearing the long dresses of the time. She had already won three women's singles titles at Wimbledon before she competed at the Olympic Games in 1900. She won a further two Wimbledon titles following Paris.

1904
ST LOUIS

This was the first Olympic Games to be held outside of Europe, and the second to be held as part of a World's Fair. The Olympic and non-Olympic events took place over a five-month period, from July to November 1904.

GAMES STATS

Opening date:
1 July 1904

Closing date:
23 November 1904

Country of host city:
United States (USA)

Nations: 12

Events: 91

This gold-plated badge was issued to honour the St Louis World's Fair.

Sticking with tradition

The 1904 Olympic Games were originally scheduled to take place in Chicago, and the St Louis World's Fair was meant to be in 1903. When the organisers of the World's Fair moved the event to 1904 instead, the International Olympic Committee (IOC) considered moving the Olympic Games to 1905, but they didn't want to break with the tradition of holding the event every four years. They eventually made the decision to combine the two events in St Louis.

A French poster for the St Louis World's Fair featuring a female figure and a Native American.

FAST FACT

The winners of the tug of war event were the American team, which was mostly made up of athletes from the Milwaukee Athletic Club.

Medals format

For the first time in 1904, the first-, second- and third-place finishers of each event received a medal. The Olympic Games in St Louis set the tradition of a gold medal for first place, silver for second place and bronze for third place that continues today.

The gold medal features a winged Victory on the globe and the bust of Zeus.

Olympic sport or not?

Many of the events of the Games were absorbed into the World's Fair programme of events and there is still debate over which ones were Olympic sports and which were not. The IOC had approved boxing, dumbbells, freestyle wrestling and the decathlon for inclusion in the Games in 1901, so there is no doubt that they were part of the 1904 Olympic Games.

Revised result

The 1904 marathon was run in such hot temperatures that only 14 of the 32 competitors finished the race. American Fred Lorz was the first to cross the finish line and fellow American Thomas Hicks claimed second place - until it was discovered that Lorz had accepted a ride in a car and only run part of the distance! Lorz was banned and Hicks won the gold.

American Frederick Winters performs in the one-hand-lift dumbbell competition. He finished in second place.

Olympic marathon winner Thomas Hicks poses with trophies he won during his career.

1908
LONDON

London hadn't been first choice for the 1908 Olympic Games - the Italian capital city of Rome was originally meant to host them. But London put on a first-rate show thanks to an impressive new multifunctional sports stadium that was built with the Games in mind.

A ticket to one of the winter sports events on the 1908 Olympic programme.

OLYMPIC GAMES OF LONDON, 1908.

SKATING COMPETITIONS.

PRINCE'S SKATING CLUB, KNIGHTSBRIDGE.

ADMIT BEARER,

THURSDAY, OCTOBER 29th, at 3 p.m.

Block A

No. 1

T.P.M.

GAMES STATS

Opening date:
27 April 1908

Closing date:
31 October 1908

Country of host city:
Great Britain (GBR)

Nations: 22

Events: 110

A railway poster advertising the Games in London, with the White City Stadium in the background.

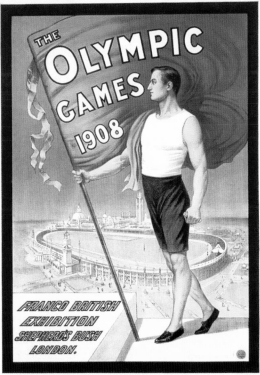

Chemin de Fer du Nord
ET
South Eastern and Chatham Railway.

THE OLYMPIC GAMES 1908

FRANCO BRITISH EXHIBITION SHEPHERD'S BUSH LONDON.

5 SERVICES RAPIDES JOURNALIERS DE PARIS À LONDRES
Via CALAIS-DOUVRES et BOULOGNE-FOLKESTONE.

White City Stadium

Even though many Olympic events took place in different venues around London and other parts of Great Britain, the centrepiece of the 1908 Games was White City Stadium in west London. The multifunctional venue was one of its kind and featured a 100-metres swimming pool within a running track which had an oval cycling track around it. The stadium had space for more than 66,000 spectators.

A dramatic finish

The 1908 marathon is best known for being Italian runner Dorando Pietri's race. Pietri was the first runner to cross the finish line, but did it in such an exhausted and dramatic way that he was disqualified from the race for being helped along by the race stewards! The second-place finisher, American Johnny Hayes, was awarded the gold medal instead.

A race official helps Italian Dorando Pietri reach the finish line of the 1908 Olympic marathon.

Lone runner

There was debate over the rules on the running track in 1908. In the 400 metres final, an American athlete blocked British athlete Wyndham Halswelle. This tactic was against the British rules, which were adopted for the Games. The race officials decided the race should be re-run two days later, but the American athletes refused to run and Wyndham Halswelle ran it alone and won the gold.

Wyndham Halswelle is the only competitor in a unique 400 metres race.

Pool hero

For the first time at the Olympic Games, swimming competitions were held in a swimming pool. The pool witnessed an impressive triple win from Henry Taylor of Great Britain. He won gold medals in the 400 metre freestyle, the 4x200 metre freestyle and the 1,500 metre freestyle – a feat that another British swimmer would not match for a century.

FAST FACT

The British organizers introduced the Olympic marathon distance we know today – 26 miles 385 yards (42,195 metres) – so their race could finish in front of the royal box at White City Stadium.

Swimmer Henry Taylor celebrates winning gold in the 4x200 metre freestyle.

THE STARS OF
ST LOUIS 1904

Many American stars shone on their own turf in the Games of the III Olympiad, with a number achieving triple victories, including Charles "Archie" Hahn. Meanwhile, track and field athlete Meyer Prinstein proved unstoppable as he made up for his disappointment four years earlier.

Charles "Archie" Hahn

Charles "Archie" Hahn, known as the Milwaukee Meteor, won the 60, 100 and 200 metres races in St Louis. Hahn grew up in a small farming town and had never set foot on a race track until he was 19. Following his triple win in the Olympic Games, Hahn turned professional, running in stunts at county fairs - including beating a racehorse over 50 yards!

Meyer Prinstein

In the 1900 Olympic Games, Meyer Prinstein had looked likely to win gold in the long jump until an official from his university banned him from competing on a Sunday, a Christian holy day, even though Prinstein was Jewish. Luckily, his qualifying jump on the Saturday was good enough to earn him second place in Paris. Four years later, nothing would stop Prinstein as he won gold in both the long jump and triple jump.

THE STARS OF
LONDON 1908

The rules of Olympic sports weren't all established or clear in 1908 - something that led to an uncomfortable victory for 400 metres runner Wyndham Halswelle and a disqualification for marathon runner Dorando Pietri.

🇬🇧 Wyndham Halswelle

Athlete Wyndham Halswelle was also a lieutenant in the British Army. He won gold in 1908 when he ran the second 400 metres final alone, His victory made him famous, but Halswelle was unhappy about how it had happened. He only ran one more race and then retired from athletics. In 1915, he died in action in the First World War.

Dorando Pietri

Dorando Pietri is perhaps more famous for the race he didn't finish than the races he did. He may not have won an Olympic gold in the 1908 marathon, but he won the hearts of the British crowds. Queen Victoria even invited him to meet her and awarded him with a gold cup for his efforts. He later proved himself to be a winning athlete as a professional – when he retired in 1911 he had won 50 of his 69 professional races.

1912
STOCKHOLM

A winner's medal from the Games in 1912.

The Swedish capital city of Stockholm hosted the Games of the V Olympiad - a competition that was filled with many technical, artistic and sporting firsts. There would not be another Olympic Games until eight years after Stockholm due to the First World War, which erupted just two years later in 1914.

GAMES STATS

Opening date:
5 May 1912

Closing date:
27 July 1912

Country of host city:
Sweden (SWE)

Nations: 28
Events: 102

The first official poster for the Olympic Games was used to advertise the event in Stockholm.

First official poster

The first official Olympic Games poster was designed for the 1912 Games by Swedish artist Olle Hjortzberg. It shows a procession of athletes each carrying their national flags. The poster was translated into 16 languages and used around the world to publicize the Games. But in certain countries the athletes' nakedness was quite shocking so the poster couldn't be used everywhere.

OLYMPISKA SPELEN
STOCKHOLM 1912
29 JUNI — 22 JULI

A. BÖRTZELLS TR. A. B STOCKHOLM

Longest wrestle

The longest wrestling match in the history of the Olympic Games took place at Stockholm 1912, lasting 11 hours and 40 minutes! In the semi-final match, Martin Klein of Russia and Alfred Asikainen of Finland wrestled to the point of exhaustion. Klein eventually won but he was so tired he couldn't wrestle in the final so his opponent, Claes Johansson of Sweden, won the gold medal.

Russia's Martin Klein wrestles Finland's Alfred Asikainen in an 11-hour wrestling semi-final.

Sports and ladders

A sports version of the board game Snakes and Ladders was produced for Stockholm 1912. It showed competitors taking part in the many sports at the Games, including athletics, fencing, cycling and show jumping, and the box featured the Stockholm Olympic Stadium. The release of the game shows how popular the Olympic Games were becoming.

An Olympic Games version of Snakes and Ladders.

The American Jim Thorpe in action in the long jump – one of the 10 sub-events in the decathlon.

Multi-discipline events

The pentathlon and decathlon athletic events were introduced for the first time in Stockholm 1912. The decathlon's sub-events are the 100 metres, 400 metres, 1,500 metres, 110 metres hurdles, long jump, high jump, pole vault, shot put, discus throw and javelin throw.

1920
ANTWERP

On short notice, the Belgian city of Antwerp hosted the 1920 Olympic Games, and athletes from around the world came together once again to compete in sporting competitions and celebrate the return of peace after the First World War.

GAMES STATS

Opening date:
20 April 1920

Closing date:
12 September 1920

Country of host city:
Belgium (BEL)

Nations: 29

Events: 154

Post-war Games

Antwerp was given the honour of hosting the Games of the VII Olympiad following the hardship the Belgian people had experienced in the First World War. There wasn't much time to prepare, but organizers quickly built an Olympic Stadium, new pools and sports halls to ensure the event was a success. A then record number of 2,626 athletes competed at the Games.

The Antwerp 1920 official poster shows the flags of the participating nations all flying together, with the city of Antwerp in the background.

FAST FACT

The official five-ringed Olympic flag flew for the first time at an Olympic Games celebration in Antwerp in 1920.

This invite to Pierre de Coubertin features the Olympic rings, which first appeared on IOC documentation in 1913.

VIIme OLYMPIADE

Le Président et les Membres du Comité Exécutif prient Monsieur le Baron P de Coubertin de leur faire l'honneur d'assister aux

Concours Olympiques

qui auront lieu au STADION à Anvers, du 14 août au 12 septembre.

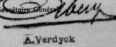

LOGE Royale

A. Verdyck

22

Tennis triumphs

French tennis player Suzanne Lenglen was one of the stars of the Games in Antwerp. She dominated the women's singles tournament, losing only four games on her way to winning Olympic gold. She also won gold in the mixed doubles tournament, and a bronze medal in the women's doubles.

Tennis star Suzanne Lenglen in action on her way to becoming an Olympic winner.

Runaway success

Albert Hill, a 31-year-old railway guard from Great Britain, surprised many when he won gold medals in the 800 and 1,500 metres races, plus a silver medal in the 3,000 metres team race. Hill's double gold achievement would not be beaten until 44 years later, when Peter Snell of New Zealand won gold in the same two events in Tokyo in 1964.

British runner Albert Hill crosses the finish line to win one of two golds in Antwerp.

Fencing hero

Nedo Nadi came as close to perfection as a fencer could get. He won five golds in Paris, and three of them were in the three fencing weapons (the foil, the épée and the sabre). He is the only fencer ever to do this at one Olympic Games.

Italian fencer Nedo Nadi with his fencing gear.

THE STARS OF
STOCKHOLM 1912

With new sports on the programme and the Olympic Games growing in popularity, there were many standout performances in Stockholm in 1912. But two stars shone brightest, with superb performances and multiple medal wins.

🇺🇸 Jim Thorpe

A tall, powerful athlete, Jim Thorpe was the top performer in four of the five pentathlon sub-events and six of the 10 decathlon sub-events in 1912. King Gustav V of Sweden said he was "the greatest athlete in the world" and awarded him a bronze statue of himself. After Stockholm, he became a professional baseball player for the New York Giants and the Cincinnati Reds.

✚ Hannes Kolehmainen

This remarkable Finnish runner won three golds and one silver medal at the 1912 Olympic Games. He also set a world record when he ran the 5,000 metres final in 14 minutes 36.6 seconds. No one had previously run it in less than 15 minutes. Hannes was the first of many great Finnish runners known as the "Flying Finns".

THE STARS OF
ANTWERP 1920

A then record number of athletes gathered to participate in the 1920 Olympic Games, and they came to win! Finland's Paavo Nurmi kicked off an impressive Olympic winning streak, while the achievements of Hawaiian Duke Kahanamoku earned him the nickname the "human fish".

 Paavo Nurmi

Paavo Nurmi was one of 12 children and worked as an errand boy before becoming the greatest runner of the first half of the 20th century. He won three gold medals at the 1920 Games, in the 10,000 metres and both the individual and team 8-kilometre cross country events. He also won silver at Antwerp and would later go on to win six more golds and two silvers at two more editions of the Olympic Games. He also set 22 official world records.

🇺🇸 Duke Kahanamoku

This double gold medal-winning swimmer had to win one of his medals twice in 1920! He won the 100 metres freestyle event for a second time after a dispute in the final meant the race had to be re-swum. He won a total of five Olympic medals and set seven world records in his career, thanks to a powerful "flutter" kick he had developed to propel his surfboard.

1924
PARIS

For the first time in its history, the modern Olympic Games returned to a city that had previously hosted the celebration. Paris was the ideal place to celebrate the 30th anniversary of the idea of the modern Olympic Games and the IOC President Pierre de Coubertin, who was about to step down from his role.

GAMES STATS

Opening date:
4 May 1924

Closing date:
27 July 1924

Country of host city:
France (FRA)

Nations: 44

Events: 126

The stuff of movies

The events of these Games inspired the 1981 Academy Award winning movie *Chariots of Fire*. Sprinters Eric Liddell and Harold Abrahams both represented Great Britain at the Games in Paris and achieved Olympic record times. Liddell won the 400 metres in 47.6 seconds and Abrahams won the 100 metres in 10.6 seconds, becoming the first European to win gold in the event.

Harold Abrahams crossing the finish line in his record-breaking 100 metres performance.

The gold medal depicts a victorious athlete offering a hand to his rival.

FAST FACT
Lane dividers in swimming competitions were added for the first time in 1924.

Long jump glory

William DeHart Hubbard became the first African American to win gold in an individual event when he triumphed in the long jump at Paris in 1924. While in the pentathlon competition, fellow American Robert LeGendre broke a long jump world record on his way to winning a bronze medal.

William DeHart Hubbard leaps to victory in the long jump competition.

Departing president

The Olympic Games were becoming more popular than ever in 1924, with lots of media stories and the first radio broadcast of the event. Pierre de Coubertin had seen the event grow from just an idea in 1892 to a popular worldwide celebration. Paris in 1924 was the last Olympic Games he oversaw. He left his role as president of the International Olympic Committee a year later, in 1925.

Pierre de Coubertin (left) walks with the Prince of Wales (centre) at the 1924 Olympic Games in Paris.

Road to Hollywood

American Johnny Weissmuller competed in swimming and water polo competitions to take home three golds and a bronze medal in 1924. Following his patricipation at the Olympics, Weissmuller put his swimming skills to use in Hollywood movies, starring as Tarzan 12 times.

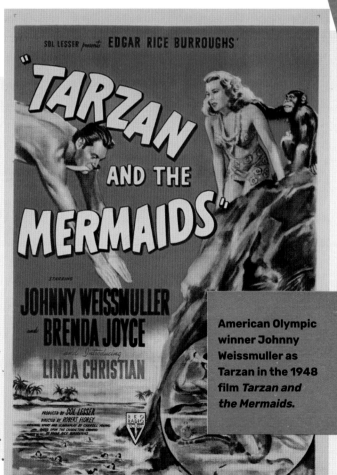

American Olympic winner Johnny Weissmuller as Tarzan in the 1948 film *Tarzan and the Mermaids*.

1928
AMSTERDAM

This was an Olympic Games that was notable for its new Opening Ceremony traditions and new sports for women, allowing more female competitors than ever before to take part.

GAMES STATS

Opening date:
17 May 1928

Closing date:
12 August 1928

Country of host city:
Netherlands (NED)

Nations: 46

Events: 109

Parade tradition

At the Opening Ceremony to the 1928 Olympic Games, competitors from around the world paraded into the stadium in alphabetical order. There were just two nations who weren't in alphabetical order: the Greek team led the parade because of their ancient Olympic connection, while the host nation's team entered the stadium last. This order is now an Olympic tradition that continues today.

An ornate diploma of merit awarded to the new IOC President Henri de Baillet-Latour.

The medal design by Giuseppe Cassioli was selected after an IOC competition.

An entrance ticket for the Opening Ceremony of the Olympic Games in Amsterdam.

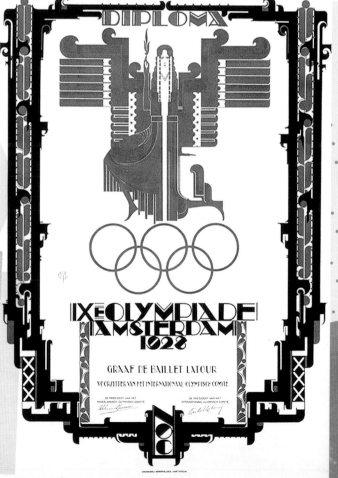

Sporting fair play

As well as medal-winning performances, there was a lot of fair play on show at the Games in Amsterdam - towards fellow competitors and even ducks! Rower Henry Pearce of Australia stopped rowing during a race to let a family of ducks pass in front of his boat. Runner Paavo Nurmi took a tumble into water during the 3,000 metres steeplechase race. France's Lucien Duquesne kindly helped him to get out!

Paavo Nurmi and Viho Ritola in the 10,000 metres race in 1928.

Ethel Catherwood of Canada became the first women's Olympic high jump champion, setting a then world record, clearing 1.59 metres.

Surprise performances

Canadian Percy Williams wasn't well known until the 1928 Olympic Games, when he did the unexpected and matched the Olympic record of 10.6 seconds for the 100 metres race. He won gold in that event and in the 200 metres. Britain's Douglas Lowe also had a surprise victory in the 800 metres, when his biggest rival, Otto Peltzer of Germany, was injured and couldn't compete in the final.

Percy Williams is carried in celebration after his victory in the 100 metres.

Female events

More women took part in these Games thanks to a larger number of events for them. A women's team gymnastics event was introduced along with five athletic competitions. In athletics, women ran the 800 metres event for the first time, but the distance was considered to be too long for women after several of the athletes collapsed. As a result, the women's 800 metres was removed from the programme until 1960.

THE STARS OF
PARIS 1924

Some of the biggest stars of the Games were also stars of the big screen. British athlete Harold Abrahams' story inspired a movie about his time at the Games, while Johnny Weissmuller followed his Olympic fame with Hollywood success. Both athletes broke Olympic records.

Harold Abrahams

Harold Abrahams was the youngest of six children and was inspired to become an athlete after his brother, Sidney, was a long jumper in the 1912 Olympic Games in Stockholm. Harold was selected for the long jump event in 1924 but he chose to take part in the sprints instead. He won a gold medal in the 100 metres and a silver in the 4 x 100 metres relay.

Johnny Weissmuller

Born in Hungary, Johnny Weissmuller grew up in the United States and learned a powerful technique for front-crawl (freestyle) swimming. He used it to win five Olympic gold medals and 24 official world records. At the 1924 Games, Johnny swam the men's 100 metres freestyle in less than one minute, and 400 metres in less than five minutes.

THE STARS OF
AMSTERDAM 1928

Two unlikely sportsmen shone at the Games - one succeeded in spite of ill health, while the other stepped out of his privileged upbringing to compete for Olympic glory. Both athletes proved themselves with winning performances.

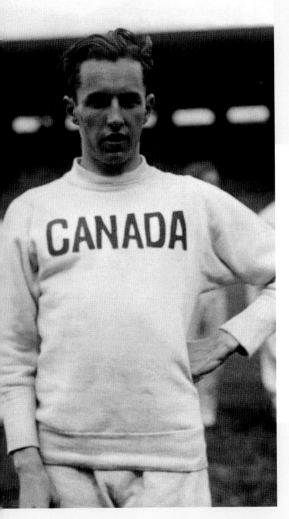

Percy Williams

Canada's first 100 metres Olympic gold medal winner was an unlikely sporting hero. He suffered rheumatic fever as a teenager and doctors said he shouldn't push himself too hard physically. But he took an interest in running. He raced a local champion and the result was a tie. He later trained hard but carefully to win a surprise double gold in the 1928 Olympic Games.

Lord David Burghley

David Burghley, later the Marquess of Exeter, was given the title Lord Burghley in 1956. He competed in three Olympic Games and won gold in the 400 metres hurdles in an Olympic record time of 53.4 seconds in 1928. Then in 1932, he won silver in the 4 x 400 metres relay. He was later a member of the International Olympic Committee and the British Parliament.

1932
LOS ANGELES

Athletes came together once again in the summer of 1932 to bring the magic of the Olympic Games to the world at the time of the Great Depression, when many people were very poor and experiencing hardship.

GAMES STATS

Opening date:
30 July 1932

Closing date:
14 August 1932

Country of host city:
United States (USA)

Nations: 37

Events: 117

Olympic village

The Olympic Organizing Committee wanted to attract athletes from around the world to the Games in Los Angeles, but they knew it would be a challenge as people didn't have a lot of money at that time. They persuaded rail and steamship companies to give cheaper fares, provided free food and created an Olympic village for the male athletes. The women stayed in hotels.

The official poster, calling for athletes to come to Los Angeles for the Games of the X Olympiad.

FAST FACT

Kusuo Kitamura of Japan, who was just 14, won gold in the 1,500 metres freestyle swimming to become the youngest-known male athlete in an individual event to win a medal.

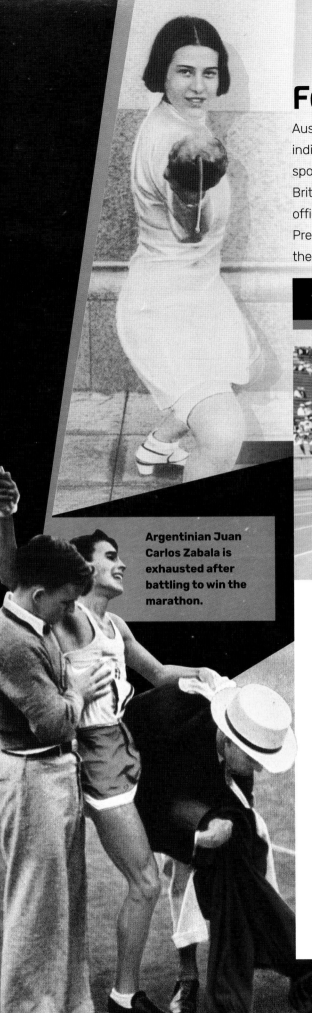

Fair fencing

Austrian Ellen Preis won gold in the women's individual foil competition thanks to the sportsmanship of her opponent, Great Britain's Heather "Judy" Guinness. When officials had failed to count two touches that Preis had scored against her, Guinness told the officials who then corrected the error.

Austrian fencer Ellen Preis, ready for action in the individual foil competition.

Finland's Lauri Lehtinen leads the 5,000 metres race.

Argentinian Juan Carlos Zabala is exhausted after battling to win the marathon.

Hollywood drama

The 5,000 metres race proved to be a fierce contest. Two Finnish runners, Lauri Lehtinen and Lauri Virtanen, took an early lead. Soon there was only one competitor left with a chance of beating them: American Ralph Hill. Lehtinen zig-zagged across the track to stop Hill from getting past him and finished just ahead for the gold. He was booed by the American crowd for his actions though!

Close run

There was a dramatic finish at the 1932 marathon, with the first four runners still closely racing one another when they entered the stadium for the final lap on the track. Argentinian runner Juan Carlos Zabala managed to hold on long enough to claim the gold medal. Great Britain's Samuel Ferris took a close second place.

1936
BERLIN

The 1936 Olympic Games witnessed the introduction of an Olympic torch relay, starting from the site of the ancient Games in Greece to Berlin. At a time of political change in Germany, the talents of the athletes shone brighter than anything else.

GAMES STATS

Opening date:
1 August 1936

Closing date:
16 August 1936

Country of host city:
Germany (GER)

Nations: 49

Events: 129

Politics and the Games

When Berlin was awarded the honour of hosting the 1936 Olympic Games back in 1931, Adolf Hitler's Nazi Party was not powerful in Germany. By 1936, Adolf Hitler was Chancellor of Germany and German symbols could be seen on the official Olympic poster and souvenirs.

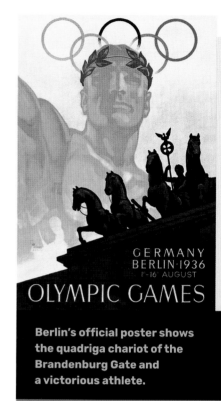

GERMANY
BERLIN·1936
1-16 AUGUST

OLYMPIC GAMES

Berlin's official poster shows the quadriga chariot of the Brandenburg Gate and a victorious athlete.

The first Olympic torch, produced in polished stainless steel.

FAST **FACT**
Basketball and handball made their first appearance in the Olympic Games in 1936 in Berlin.

Viewing rooms

In addition to attending events in the venues, for the first time at an Olympic celebration, people had the chance to watch without a ticket. There were television viewing rooms that people could go to free of charge to catch all of the action, allowing more people than ever before to see the Games.

Marjorie Gestring diving from the 3 metres springboard to win gold.

Fans filled the Olympic stadium in Berlin to cheer on the athletes.

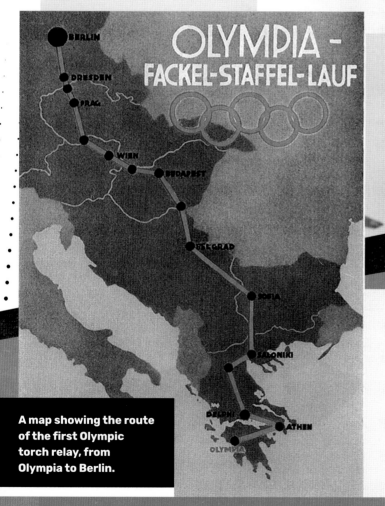

OLYMPIA – FACKEL-STAFFEL-LAUF

A map showing the route of the first Olympic torch relay, from Olympia to Berlin.

Diving for gold

American Marjorie Gestring won a gold medal in the 1936 diving competitions and became the youngest-ever female to win a gold medal. She was just 13 years and 268 days old when she leapt to victory from the 3 metres springboard.

Torch relay

The very first Olympic torch relay was run in 1936. The idea to have a relay was inspired by Ancient Greek torch races. The torch was lit from the rays of the sun at Olympia, the site of the ancient Games. It was carried by runners in a relay race from Olympia to Berlin, a journey that took 12 days.

THE STARS OF
LOS ANGELES
1932

Multi-talented athletes defined the Games in 1932. Eddie Tolan defied expectations by taking the top spot on the Olympic podium twice. And Babe Didrikson proved herself to be among the best all-round athletes of all time.

 ## Mildred "Babe" Didrikson

A true sporting talent, Babe Didrikson took part in eight events at the 1932 US Olympic trials and won six. She was only allowed to enter three events in the Olympic Games, but won medals in all three! She won gold in both the 80 metres hurdles and the javelin competition, then took the silver medal after a dramatic "jump-off" in the high jump final.

 ## Thomas "Eddie"

Thomas "Eddie" Tolan dreamed of becoming a Football player, but his relatively short height metres stopped him from competing in the s Tolan concentrated on running and triumped Olympic 100 metres race. He matched the w 10.3 seconds in his medal-winning race, and another victory in the 200 metres in Los Ang

THE STARS OF
BERLIN 1936

Amid Germany's political backdrop, it was African-American sprinter and long jumper Jesse Owens who emerged as the most popular athlete in Berlin. Meanwhile, the 1,500 metre race produced another hero in New Zealand's John Lovelock.

 ## Jesse Owens

Jesse Owens was a huge star of Berlin 1936. He won gold medals in the 100 metres, 200 metres, the long jump and the 4 x 100 metres relay. Born in Alabama, he was the youngest of 10 children and was christened James Cleveland Owens. A schoolteacher misheard him when he said his name was "J. C. Owens" and he was known as Jesse ever after.

John Lovelock

John Lovelock became New Zealand's first Olympic champion in 1936, in the 1,500 metres race. In a fiercely fought final, Lovelock beat American Glenn Cunningham to the gold medal. Both competitors broke the world record, and the three competitors who finished behind them broke the Olympic record!

1948
LONDON

Engraved with the Olympic rings, this standard torch was made of stainless steel.

Two Olympic Games editions had been cancelled in 1940 and 1944 because of the Second World War. In 1948, the Olympics returned once again to London to bring athletes of the world together.

Olympic effort

In 1948 Great Britain was still recovering from the Second World War, so there was a shortage of places to stay, food and equipment. Olympic organizers had to be creative with what they already had. They used existing sports venues instead of building new ones. They arranged for athletes to stay in army camps, schools and hotels. And many countries gave gifts of food – Denmark donated 160,000 eggs!

The official poster of the Games of the XIV Olympiad shows Big Ben and the Houses of Parliament.

A starters' pistol and a camera used at the 1948 Games.

GAMES STATS

Opening date:
29 July 1948

Closing date:
14 August 1948

Country of host city:
Great Britain (GBR)

Nations: 59

Events: 136

New technology

The world had changed since the last Olympic celebration and there were new technologies that could help both organizers and athletes in sporting events. Starting blocks were used for the first time, to help runners have faster starts. The starters' pistol, which signals the start of a race, was linked to an electronic race timer. And a camera could be used to decide on the winner of a close finish.

Decathlon newcomer

American Robert Mathias had first completed a decathlon only three months before he entered as a contestant at the 1948 Games. He didn't have it easy – bad weather delayed the start of the decathlon, and it was so dark for the last two events that they had to be lit by car lights! Neverthless, Mathius won gold and became the youngest ever decathlon champion at age 17.

British gymnast Ken Buffin executes a flying backroll on the parallel bars at the Empress Hall at London's Earl's Court.

FAST FACT

Károly Takács of Hungary lost his right hand in army training but he was able to use his left hand to win the rapid-fire pistol competition in 1948 (and again in 1952).

Quick adjustments

Olympic organizers and athletes showed how well they could adapt at the Games in London to make the competitions a success. For example, competitors in the cycling who finished late wore white vests to remain visible in the dark! In the gymnastics events, wet weather and mud meant the events had to be moved to an indoor venue at the last minute.

1952
HELSINKI

Finland's capital city Helsinki was the smallest city to host the Olympic Games but that didn't stop athletes from producing big results there.

New Opportunity

It was Helsinki's second chance to host the Olympic Games when they finally did it in 1952. Helsinki had also been given the honour of hosting them in 1940, when Tokyo in Japan had to pull out of hosting it due to war. In the end, the 1940 Games were cancelled altogether, but Helsinki had already built some Olympic venues for 1940, including cycling and swimming stadiums, that they could finally use!

The official 1952 poster was first created for the 1940 Games before they were cancelled.

FAST FACT

The first coin celebrating the Olympic Games was created for the 1952 Games. 600,000 coins, showing a laurel wreath and the Olympic rings, were issued.

Only 22 Olympic torches were made for the 1952 Games.

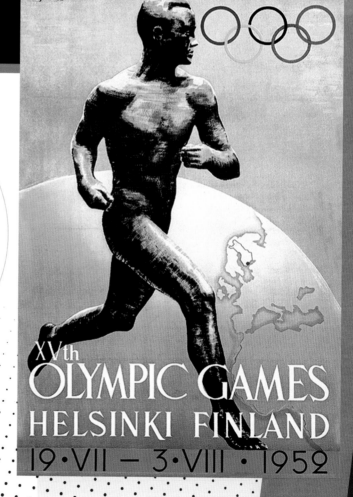

SUOMI · FINLAND 500 MARKKAA

XVth OLYMPIC GAMES HELSINKI FINLAND
19 · VII — 3 · VIII · 1952

A guide to one of the campsites for Olympic guests in Helsinki.

Olympic camping

Places to stay to enjoy or participate in the Games of the XV Olympiad were in short supply in Finland. Campsites were specially created to house spectators at the Games. The Olympic organizers also built new housing for the athletes and even created a separate village for athletes from the Soviet Union, which was the name for Russia at the time, as well as for athletes from other Eastern European countries.

Two cauldrons

Helsinki added their own twist to the Olympic torch relay. They had two final torch bearers in the stadium for the Opening Ceremony instead of one. The reason for the double honour was Finland couldn't choose which of its greatest athletes to give it to! Long-distance runners Paavo Nurmi and Hannes Kolehmainen were both legends.

Brazilian record breaker

Adhemar Ferreira Da Silva hopped, stepped and jumped his way into the record books in the triple jump event and was the only Brazilian athlete to win a gold medal at 1952 Olympic Games. He won the event with an Olympic and world record distance of 16.22 metres.

Brazilian Adhemar Ferreira Da Silva in action during the triple-jump competition.

Paavo Nurmi lights the cauldron located on the track in the stadium.

41

THE STARS OF
LONDON 1948

Among the biggest stars of London in 1948 was an Olympic newcomer, while another returned to Olympic competition after a 12-year gap. Both Emil Zátopek and Fanny Blankers-Koen entered the history books as two of the world's greatest athletes.

Emil Zátopek

One of the best long-distance runners ever, Emil Zátopek won his first Olympic gold medal at London 1948 with a victory in the 10,000 metres race. He lapped most of his opponents and finished with a lead of more than 300 metres! Later, at the 1952 Olympic Games, he won the 5,000 and 10,000 metres races and the marathon. No runner has ever achieved the same triple win.

Fanny Blankers-Koen

Fanny Blankers-Koen had competed in Berlin in 1936 and returned to the Games in London 12 years later to win four gold medals! She had victories in the 100 metres, 80 metres hurdles, the 4 x 100 metres relay race and the newly introduced women's 200 metres race. During her incredible career, she set 16 world records in eight different events.

THE STARS OF
HELSINKI 1952

Unbeatable athletes graced the track and field events of the 1952 Olympic Games. Marjorie Jackson was queen of the women's sprint events, while the American Bob Mathias successfully defended his decathlon crown.

Marjorie Jackson

Australia's Marjorie Jackson was a star of the sprint events in Helsinki, winning gold medals in the 100 and 200 metres races. She was so fast she earned the nickname the "Lithglow flash", after the Australian town where she grew up. She went unbeaten from 1950 to 1954, and broke 18 world records!

Robert "Bob" Mathias

After winning Olympic gold in the decathlon in London in 1948, Robert "Bob" Mathias won gold in the event again in 1952 - this time with a world record-breaking score of 7,887 points. He was the first athlete ever to defend the decathlon title in a second Olympic Games. When he retired from sport, Bob Mathias became a politician and was later the first director of the US Olympic Training Centre.

1956
MELBOURNE AND STOCKHOLM

For the first time the Olympic Games were held in two different countries, on two different continents and at two different times of the year.

GAMES STATS

Opening date:
22 November 1956

Closing date:
8 December 1956

Country of host city:
Australia (AUS)

Nations: 67

Events: 145

Two countries

When Melbourne was chosen as the host of the Games of the XVI Olympiad, no one anticipated that Australian laws would become a problem for the equestrian events. There were strict laws on what could go in and out of the country, including horses. So the International Olympic Committee decided to hold the equestrian competitions in the Swedish city of Stockholm in June 1956.

This bronze plate shows the emblem that was created for the Olympic equestrian events in Stockholm.

Kangaroo cameo

To celebrate the Olympic Games being held Down Under for the first time, a kangaroo appeared within the iconic Olympic rings! It was part of the city of Melbourne's coat of arms shield. It can be seen on this Cadbury's chocolate box created for the Games, along with a picture of the Melbourne skyline.

Winners in the water

In the Melbourne swimming pool, Australian athletes proved why freestyle swimming is also known as the "Australian crawl". The female swimmers took gold, silver and bronze in the freestyle 100 metres competition, and the male swimmers did the same in their event. Fellow Aussie Murray Rose also won gold in the 400 and 1,500 metres freestyle races.

Swimmers are poised to take to the pool in the men's 400 metres freestyle race.

Australia's Shirley Strickland going for gold in the 80 metres hurdles final.

FAST FACT

East and West Germany came together to form a team called the "United Team of Germany" for the 1956 Games.

This torch was used for the last runner during the torch relay in Melbourne.

Track triumphs

Australia's team of athletes also did well on the running track. Shirley Strickland won the 80 metres hurdles in a new Olympic record time of 10.8 seconds. Meanwhile, 18-year-old Betty Cuthbert won triple gold medals, in the 100 and 200 metres races and the 4 x 100 relay race. A feat that earned her the nickname of Australia's "golden girl".

1960
ROME

Rome got a second chance to host the Olympic Games after having to pull out of holding them in 1908. Second time around, the celebration in Rome mixed beautiful historical monuments with modern sporting venues.

GAMES STATS

Opening date:
25 August 1960

Closing date:
11 September 1960

Country of host city:
Italy (ITA)

Nations: 83

Events: 150

Ancient and modern

Rome is a city filled with ancient monuments that once played host to Roman sports. The wrestling events at the 1960 Olympic Games took place in the vaults of an ancient Roman building called the Basilica of Maxentius. This history blended with the sleek, modern design of a brand-new Olympic Stadium called Palazzetto dello Sport (which means "Small Sport Palace" in English) that was specially built for the 1960 Games.

FAST FACT

The Olympic Games reached more people in the world than ever before thanks to television.

The design of the torch was inspired by the torches reproduced on ancient monuments.

The official poster reflects the old and new styles that were highlighted for the Games in Rome.

JEUX DE LA XVII OLYMPIADE

ROMA   25.VIII–11.IX

ROMA   MCMLX

Medal chain

For the first time in 1960, Olympic medal winners could easily wear their medals. The medals were set in a laurel wreath circle and attached to a matching chain.

A medal and laurel wreath chain from the Rome 1960 Olympic Games.

Peder Lunde Jr in action in the sailing competition.

Olympic family

Olympic history was made when Norway's Peder Lunde Jr won a gold medal in the Flying Dutchman yachting competition. His father, also named Peder, had won silver in 1952 and his grandfather, Eugene, had won gold in 1924. This is the only time a grandfather, father and son have all won medals in the same Olympic sport.

Friendly rivalry

Friends Chuan-Kwang Yang of Chinese Taipei and Rafer Johnson of the United States competed in a very close decathlon competition. Yang won the last of the 10 sub-events – the 1,500 metres - but Johnson had just scored enough points in the other sub-events to win gold while Yang took home the silver medal.

American Rafer Johnson throws the shot put on his way to winning the decathlon.

THE STARS OF
MELBOURNE AND
STOCKHOLM 1956

Five months after the equestrian events in Stockholm, 3,155 athletes came to Melbourne to compete in 145 events. They made Olympic history and broke world records.

Dawn Fraser

Dawn Fraser won the women's 100 metres freestyle event at the 1956 Olympic Games – and would go on to win the same event at two more editions of the Games, in 1960 and 1964. She is one of only three swimmers ever to win the same event at three Games, one after the other. She also won silver in the 400 metres freestyle in 1956, and a gold and three silvers in relay events.

 ## Vladimir Kuts

Despite never running a race until he was 21, Vladmir Kuts defied the odds at the 1956 Games. In his only Olympic appearance, he won both the 5,000 and 10,000 metres races – and set a world record in the 10,000 metres.

THE STARS OF
ROME 1960

American boxer Cassius Clay, who would go on to become a sporting icon, lit up the Games in Rome. It was also in Rome that Ethiopian runner Abebe Bikila conquered the cobbled streets of the city to win gold in the marathon.

 ## Abebe Bikila

Abebe Bikila ran the uneven, cobbled streets of Rome barefoot to win gold in the 1960 marathon. Bikila had brought new shoes to run in but they weren't comfortable, so he decided to run without them. He even managed to break the world record. He was also the first sub-Saharan African ever to win an Olympic gold medal.

 ## Cassius Clay

Cassius Clay, who later changed his name to Muhammad Ali, made his only appearance in the Olympic boxing ring in 1960 at the age of 18. He confidently told everyone he would win the gold medal - and he did. He became a professional boxer and went on to win the world heavyweight championship three times. He is widely regarded as one of the greatest boxers of all time.

1964
TOKYO

The Olympic Games were held in Asia for the first time when Tokyo welcomed the world to a new, modern Japan. Also for the first time, TV audiences around the world enjoyed the sporting action in colour.

The Tokyo torch was made of aluminium to make it light and easy to carry.

GAMES STATS

Opening date:
10 October 1964

Closing date:
24 October 1964

Country of host city:
Japan (JPN)

Nations: 93

Events: 163

Eastern excitement

Japan was introduced to the Games and its symbols in 1964. The Japanese people were so excited about the celebration that they bought more than 1.8 million tickets to the events. When the Olympic flame reached Japan, it was divided into four torches that took four different routes around the country to allow as many Japanese people as possible to see it.

An entry ticket from the 1964 Games in Tokyo.

Judo first

Judo was an Olympic sport for the first time in Tokyo because of its Japanese roots. Many of Japan's athletes shone in those events. Takehide Nakatani, Isao Inokuma and Isao Okano each won gold. But in one surprise result, Antonius "Anton" Geesink of the Netherlands took gold from Japan's Akio Kaminaga.

The Netherlands' Anton Geesink on his way to judo victory in Tokyo.

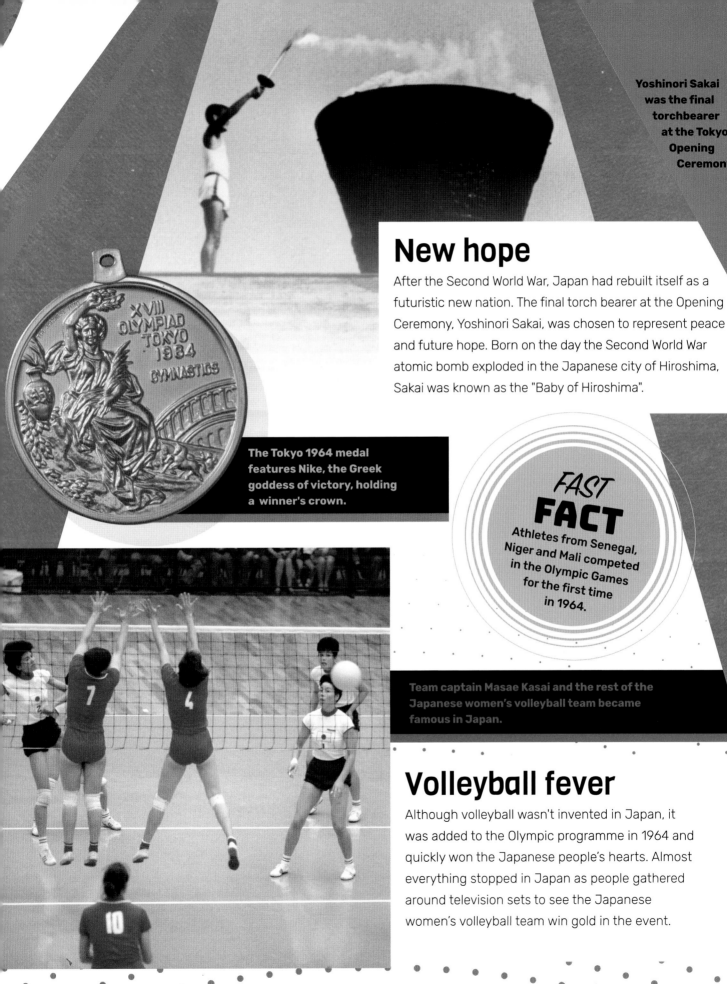

Yoshinori Sakai was the final torchbearer at the Tokyo Opening Ceremony.

New hope

After the Second World War, Japan had rebuilt itself as a futuristic new nation. The final torch bearer at the Opening Ceremony, Yoshinori Sakai, was chosen to represent peace and future hope. Born on the day the Second World War atomic bomb exploded in the Japanese city of Hiroshima, Sakai was known as the "Baby of Hiroshima".

The Tokyo 1964 medal features Nike, the Greek goddess of victory, holding a winner's crown.

FAST FACT
Athletes from Senegal, Niger and Mali competed in the Olympic Games for the first time in 1964.

Team captain Masae Kasai and the rest of the Japanese women's volleyball team became famous in Japan.

Volleyball fever

Although volleyball wasn't invented in Japan, it was added to the Olympic programme in 1964 and quickly won the Japanese people's hearts. Almost everything stopped in Japan as people gathered around television sets to see the Japanese women's volleyball team win gold in the event.

1968
MEXICO CITY

The Games of the XIX Olympiad in Mexico City were memorable for their joyful and colourful spirit. What's more, the city's high altitude added drama to the competition, proving an advantage in some events while a disadvantage in others.

GAMES STATS

Opening date:
12 October 1968

Closing date:
27 October 1968

Country of host city:
Mexico (MEX)

Nations: 112

Events: 172

The tickets and uniforms for Mexico 1968 reflected the graphic look adopted for the Games.

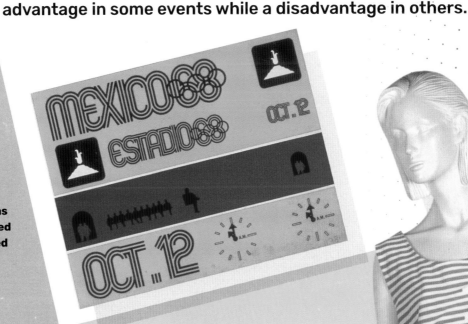

This torch was among the three types used for the 1968 Olympic torch relay.

Arts festival

For the first time in Olympic history, the organizers decided to hold an arts festival, which lasted longer than the Games. There were more than 500 Mexican and international events celebrating dance, poetry, science, art and architecture. There was even a festival of children's painting and a film festival. The design for the events of the 1968 Games as well as for items such as posters, uniforms and torches all had a striking, artistic look.

High altitude

Mexico City's location high above sea level was a challenge for the athletes of the 1968 Games. Endurance sports such as the marathon became harder at a high altitude, but it seemed to have a positive effect on other events. An eight-year world record was broken five times in the men's triple jump. In the 400 metres race, American Lee Evans set a world record of 43.85 seconds that would last 20 years!

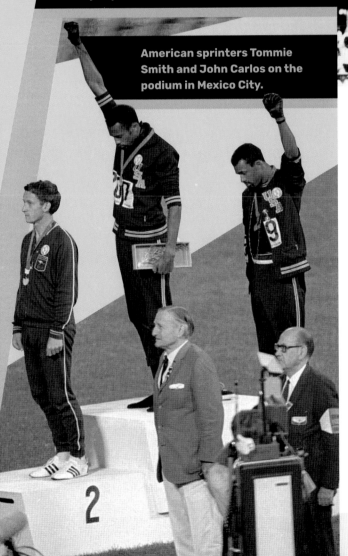

Viktor Saneyev representing the USSR competes in the men's triple jump event.

American sprinters Tommie Smith and John Carlos on the podium in Mexico City.

Dick Fosbury performing his "flop", which introduced a new technique for high jumping.

Evolutionary jump

American Richard "Dick" Fosbury used a new technique in the high jump that changed the way athletes competed in the event forever after. Fosbury twisted around after he took off from the ground so he flew over the bar head and back first. His new technique was known as the "Fosbury flop" and it won him the gold medal.

Political protest

American sprinters Tommie Smith and John Carlos, who won gold and bronze in the 200 metres race, each raised a black-gloved fist when they stood on the winners' podium. It was a gesture called the "Black Power" salute. They did it to protest against the poor treatment of black people in America.

THE STARS OF
TOKYO 1964

More than 5,000 athletes from 93 countries competed in Tokyo. Most notably, the swimming events boasted new Olympic records in every event and a dozen world records, thanks in part to the feats of the USA's Don Schollander. Meanwhile, gymnast Larisa Latynina ended her Olympic career with gold-medal performances.

Larisa Latynina

Larisa Latynina trained as a ballet dancer from age 11 before moving into gymnastics, where she became one of the greatest Olympic gymnasts of all time. Latynina won two gold medals at the Games in Tokyo, adding to the seven medals she had already won in Melbourne and Rome. She won a total of 18 Olympic medals in her career – a record for a female Olympian in any sport at the Games.

Donald "Don" Schollander

Swimmer Don Schollander became the first American to win four gold medals at a single Olympic Games since Jesse Owens had done the same in 1936. His four victories in Tokyo came in 100 and 400 metres freestyle races and the 4 x 100 and 4 x 200 metres freestyle relay events.

THE STARS OF
MEXICO CITY 1968

The high altitude in Mexico City was expected to be a challenge for the Olympic competitors, but in the athletic sprint and jumping events it might have been the reason for some athletes' outstanding results that remained world records for decades.

🇺🇸 James "Jim" Hines

Jim Hines won the 100 metres gold medal and broke the world record with a time of 9.95 seconds. His new record would not be broken for 15 years! Hines did not believe that high altitude helped him to reach such an amazing time. He took home another gold medal in the 4 x 100 metres relay. After the Games, he became a professional football player for the Miami Dophins.

🇺🇸 Bob Beamon

Bob Beamon's long jump was one of the incredible moments of the Games in Mexico City. He jumped so far that the automatic measuring device slid off its rail before it could record his jump! Officials had to call for a measuring tape to measure the length of the jump, which was a massive 8.90 metres! He had improved on the world record by 55 centimetres. His record wasn't beaten for the next 23 years.

1972
MUNICH

The 1972 Olympic Games were a mixture of triumph and tragedy. Athletes proved they could overcome anything by achieving amazing results even though the Games sadly did not go as planned.

Made by the firm Krupp, Munich's Olympic torch could burn for up to 22 minutes.

GAMES STATS

Opening date:
26 August 1972

Closing date:
11 September 1972

Country of host city:
Federal Republic of Germany (FRG)

Nations: 121

Events: 195

Celebrations and sadness

The organizers of Munich 1972 had planned for the Games to be a joyful and colourful celebration. They had built a futuristic Olympic Stadium in Munich to host the Games. But joy turned to sadness when a group of terrorists entered the Olympic Village and killed two members of the Israeli delegation and kidnapped nine more. They were all later killed along with a German policeman. The Games were temporarily halted and a memorial service held.

Flowers outside the building where members of the Israeli delegation died.

FAST FACT

Waldi the Dachshund was the first official summer mascot of the Olympic Games.

München 1972 26.8.–10.9.

The official Munich poster featured the modern design of the new Olympic Stadium.

Making waves

A state-of-the-art swimming pool in Munich, with new ripple-reducing lane markers, was made for record-breaking moments. American swimmer Mark Spitz was responsible for many of them, winning an incredible seven golds and breaking world records to win each one. In the women's events, Shane Gould of Australia, who was only 15 years old, won three gold medals in world-record time.

Mark Spitz swims his way to gold in Munich.

Shark shoes

Kipchoge "Kip" Keino broke the 3,000 metres steeplechase Olympic record wearing special shoes (above). The sole had been cut in places and some shark skin was added. This was supposed to help the shoes grip better when they were underwater, during the water jump part of the steeplechase.

Ulrike Mayfarth with her gold medal for the women's high jump event.

Young leap

Ulrike Meyfarth of the Federal Republic of Germany jumped higher than she had ever jumped before in Munich, clearing 1.92 metres to set a new Olympic record. At 16 years old, Meyfarth also became the youngest person ever to win an individual athletics gold medal. Twelve years later in 1984, she would win gold again in Los Angeles.

1976
MONTREAL

The Games of the XXI Olympiad was the first and, so far, only Summer Games edition to be held in Canada. Although many African nations chose not to take part in protest, once the Games were underway, athletes delivered some podium-worthy Olympic moments.

GAMES STATS

Opening date:
17 July 1976

Closing date:
1 August 1976

Country of host city:
Canada (CAN)

Nations: 92
Events: 198

The Invitation

The official poster for the 1976 Olympic Games shows the five iconic Olympic rings moving from different directions into the centre of the poster. Named "The Invitation", the poster features the five rings reflected symbolically by a series of waves, which invite athletes across the world to take part in the Games.

FAST
FACT
Amik the beaver was the Montreal mascot. Its name was taken from the Algonquin language.

Montréal 1976

58

Perfect 10

One of the biggest moments in Olympic gymnastics history came at the Games when a 14-year-old Romanian gymnast named Nadia Comaneci scored the maximum 10 points on the uneven bars. This result, which had never been achieved before, was so unexpected that officials discovered they could not display "10.00" on the scoreboard. Instead, Comaneci's incredible score was displayed as 1.00.

Romania's Nadia Comaneci puts on a perfect performance at the 1976 Olympic Games.

Flame innovation

The Olympic torch relay was a little different in 1976. The Olympic flame travelled from Greece to Canada by air, but not in a plane. It was carried by relay from Olympia to Athens, where it was transformed into a coded impulse and sent to the Canadian capital of Ottawa. In Ottawa, a laser beam was used to change the flame back into its original fiery form.

The two final torch bearers were young Canadians representing the nation's French and English heritage.

Miklos Nemeth celebrates his gold-medal-winning javelin throw in 1976.

Throwing for gold

Hungarian javelin thrower Miklos Nemeth was overjoyed to set a new world-record javelin throw of 94.58 metres. He was even more excited to repeat his father Imre's winning performance in the hammer throw competition in 1948. Both Miklos and his father won gold in the event.

THE STARS OF
MUNICH 1972

Out of the dark moments of the Games in Munich emerged some big, shining stars. American swimmer Mark Spitz finally achieved his ambitions and probably even surpassed them! And Soviet Union gymnast Olga Korbut won medals as well as the hearts of the spectators.

Olga Korbut

Gymnast Olga Korbut was small in stature but she made a big impression on the crowds at the 1972 Olympic Games. Her spectacular routines made her one of the stars in Munich. She won two individual gold medals as well as a gold in the team competition. She was so popular, she had to don a disguise when she visited the shops in the city so that she wouldn't draw attention.

Mark Spitz

Following personal disappointment over his performance in Mexico City in 1968, Mark Spitz did what no athlete had done before. At the Games in Munich he won seven Olympic gold medals in a single Games edition. Over his entire career, he won 10 Olympic medals (nine gold) and set 26 world records.

THE STARS OF
MONTREAL 1976

Two stars of Montreal made sporting history that would remain in the record books to this day. One achieved a score that had never seen before, while the other reluctantly ran a race to win a double gold that has never been repeated.

Nadia Comaneci

After becoming the first gymnast ever to score a perfect 10 in the Olympic Games on the uneven bars, Nadia scored another six perfect 10s in Montreal! She won the women's individual all-round title, and took home golds in the uneven bars and the balance beam. She achieved a total of nine Olympic medals in her career, and five of them were gold.

Alberto Juantorena

Cuban athlete Alberto Juantorena is the only man in Olympic history to win gold medals in both the 400 and 800 metres. At 1.90 metres tall, he had a giant stride that meant he made a big impact in the track events. However, his coach had to persuade him to run the 800 metres by telling him it would be good practice for the 400 metres race, which Juantorena much preferred!

1980
MOSCOW

A US-led boycott resulted in fewer participants in Moscow, but the athletes who did attend the 1980 Games still produced many outstanding performances and magical moments.

GAMES STATS

Opening date:
19 July 1980

Closing date:
3 August 1980

Country of host city:
Soviet Union (URS)

Nations: 80
Events: 203

Olympic boycott

Although the world's athletes had prepared for the 1980 Games, a large number of them didn't take part. When the Soviet Union invaded Afghanistan, the US president, Jimmy Carter, called on the world not to attend the celebration in protest. Those athletes who did come were in superb form and together broke more records than in Montreal four years earlier.

A group of scientists designed the 1980 Olympic torch in just two months.

Ever-changing mosaic scenes like the one below also featured at the Opening Ceremony for the 1980 Games.

FAST **FACT**

Misha the Bear, the Games' mascot, was chosen by 40,000 viewers of a television programme.

Eight medals

The biggest star of the gymnastics competitions was Aleksandr Dityatin of the Soviet Union. He won the all-round individual event, plus two more gold medals in the team and rings events. He also won four silver medals in the horizontal bar, parallel bars, pommel horse and vault competitions, as well as a bronze in the floor exercises. No other gymnast has ever won so many medals in one Games edition.

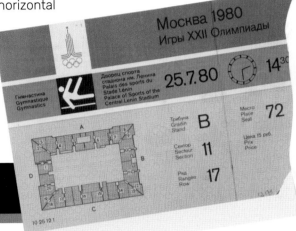

Aleksandr Dityatin poised to win gold in the rings event.

A ticket to the gymnastics competitions in Moscow.

Emblem art

The Games' emblem, which featured on several different posters for Moscow, appeared in various creative forms. Originally the emblem was inspired by both the lanes of a running track as well as the buildings of Moscow, but one poster artist decided to add flames to the design and make it look like a rocket launching into space.

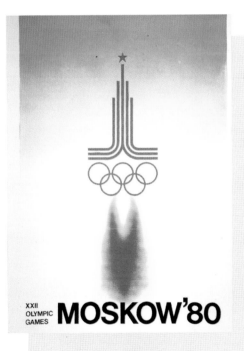

XXII OLYMPIC GAMES **MOSKOW'80**

Teófilo Stevenson competing to win his Olympic gold.

Triple gold

In his third Olympic Games, Cuban boxer Teófilo Stevenson became a sporting legend. He won the heavyweight contest to capture a third Olympic gold medal. He became only the second boxer in Olympic history to win three golds, and the first to have won them in consecutive Games in the same weight category.

1984
LOS ANGELES

The Olympic Games returned to Los Angeles after 52 years. Once again the American city brought its unique Hollywood style to the sporting celebration.

The torch shows a peristyle of the Los Angeles Memorial Coliseum.

It's showtime!

The Opening Ceremony of the 1984 Olympic Games quickly set the festive atmosphere of the celebration. It was a musical extravaganza that included 85 pianos, a "rocket man" in a jet-propelled backpack, and spectators using cards to create a huge display of the flags of the participating countries.

The glittering Opening Ceremony of Los Angeles 1984.

GAMES STATS

Opening date:
28 July 1984

Closing date:
12 August 1984

Country of host city:
United States (USA)

Nations: 140

Events: 221

The American eagle mascot Sam symbolised optimism.

FAST **FACT**

Two women's synchronised swimming events were added to the Olympic sports programme in 1984.

Financial success

Unlike previous Olympic Games, the Los Angeles event wasn't funded by the government so organizers had to find other ways to pay for the event. In the end, many companies became sponsors and in return were allowed to advertise at the Games. Organizers also held the event at existing venues to save on building costs. The Games made more than $200m profit.

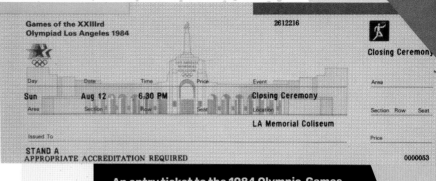

An entry ticket to the 1984 Olympic Games Closing Ceremony.

Gold feet

American athlete Carl Lewis added a touch of gold to his footwear to help him to win a gold medal in the 200 metres race. It was one of Lewis' four victories at the Games that helped him match the 1936 Olympic achievement of fellow American Jesse Owens. Like Owens, Lewis won gold medals in the 100 and 200 metres, the long jump and the 4 x 100 metres relay.

Carl Lewis in action in his gold-trimmed running shoes.

Going the distance

Back in 1928, the distance of 800 metres had been thought of as too far for women to race. By 1984, times were very different and that year's Games saw the introduction of an Olympic marathon for women. American runner Joan Benoit became the first female champion of the event. Her time of two hours, 24 minutes and 52 seconds would have won a gold medal in 13 of the 19 men's Olympic marathons that had been run before 1984.

THE STARS OF
MOSCOW 1980

Only 80 nations might have taken part in Moscow, but there was no shortage of drama. Steve Ovett experienced a surprise twist of fate, while Miruts Yifter finally achieved his Olympic gold dream.

Miruts Yifter

Ethiopian distance runner Miruts Yifter stormed to gold in both the 5,000 and 10,000 metres in Moscow in 1980. He won his races with such fast finishes he was nicknamed "Yifter the Shifter"! He had waited some time to win gold. In 1972, he won bronze in the 10,000 metres, but in 1976 his country decided not to take part in Montreal.

Steve Ovett

Great Britain's Steve Ovett was expected to win the 1,500 metres in Moscow, as he had been unbeaten in the event for three years. His rival and fellow Briton, Sebastian Coe, was expected to win the 800 metres. In an unexpected twist, Ovett won the 800 metres and Coe captured the 1,500 metres title.

THE STARS OF
LOS ANGELES 1984

As more women's competitions entered the Olympic programme in 1984 and made new stars of their winners, the men's competitions were celebrated as much for their links to Olympic history as they were for new achievements.

Sebastian "Seb" Coe

Seb Coe won the gold medal in the 1,500 metres race in Los Angeles, just as he had done in Moscow four years earlier. As a result, Coe became the only athlete to have defended an Olympic 1,500 metres title. He also won two silver medals in the 800 metres at the Games in 1980 and 1984..

Mary Lou Retton

This American gymnast stole the show and won the women's all-round individual gymnastics title in Los Angeles. Retton made use of her muscle power to impress the judges and scored perfect 10s in the floor and vault events. As well as her gold medal, Mary Lou also took home silvers in the vault and team events and bronze medals in the uneven bars and floor events.

1988
SEOUL

The Olympic Games went back to Asia, this time to the South Korean capital city of Seoul. They were a celebration of Korean culture with many memorable moments, including the return of tennis to the Games.

The Seoul Olympic torch features Korean motifs of the signs of the Zodiac.

GAMES STATS

Opening date:
7 September 1988

Closing date:
2 October 1988

Country of host city:
Republic of Korea (KOR)

Nations: 159
Events: 237

A participant's medal shows the Namdaemun, the "southern gate" – a Korean landmark built in the 14th century.

Seoul Ceremony

The Opening Ceremony celebrated Korean tradition and a sporting hero. The Ceremony began with a large Korean dragon drum that was brought along the nearby River Han and then into the stadium. Sohn Kee-chung who had won gold in the Olympic marathon in 1936 (competing under the Japanese name Kitei Son) carried the Olympic flame into the stadium to the delight of the spectators.

FAST FACT

To everyone's surprise, Anthony Nesty of Suriname - a small country where there was only one Olympic-size swimming pool - beat American swimming star Matt Biondi in the men's 100 metres butterfly event.

The dragon drum enters the Olympic Stadium in Seoul.

All-seasons athlete

Christa Luding-Rothenburger of the German Democratic Republic won silver in the cycling 1,000 metres match sprint in Seoul. The race came just seven months after she won gold and silver in the speed-skating events at the 1988 Olympic Winter Games. With her achievement in Seoul she became the only athlete to win medals at both the Summer and Winter Games in the same year.

Tiger mascots

Hodori was the tiger mascot of the Games in Seoul while Hosuni was his female counterpart. In Korea, the tiger is a legendary animal that represents bravery. "Ho" means tiger, "dori" means little boy and "suni" means little girl.

Christa Luding-Rothenburger in action in the final of the women's cycling 1,000 metres match sprint.

Professional Steffi Graf won Olympic gold in the women's singles tennis title.

Tennis returns

Tennis returned to the Olympics in 1988, 64 years after it had been removed from the Olympic sports programme. This time round, professional athletes were allowed to take part. But in order to compete, the professionals had to embrace the Olympic experience by living in the Olympic Village and soaking up the atmosphere - not just playing for gold.

1992
BARCELONA

When the Olympic Games came to Barcelona in 1992, they brought new beauty, buildings and transport links to the city that its citizens could enjoy for years to come.

GAMES STATS

Opening date:
25 July 1992

Closing date:
9 August 1992

Country of host city:
Spain (ESP)

Nations: 169

Events: 259

Olympic legacies

Olympic organizers in Barcelona revamped parts of the city so it could host a fabulous celebration. The waterfront area was transformed and sports venues were newly built or updated for use both during the Games and thereafter. Roads and railway lines were also built to make venues easy to reach and bring positive changes for the future of the city.

The design of the 1992 Olympic torch reflected a more modern style.

Figurine of the 1992 Olympic Games' mascot, Cobi the "crazy" dog, playing football.

Barcelona'92

© 1988 COOB'92, S.A. All rights reserved TM

This poster shows the official emblem of the Games in Barcelona.

All-star team

With professional athletes now allowed to take part in more sports at the Olympic Games, the USA brought their best to the basketball competition of Barcelona. Their American "dream team" of players included superstars Earvin "Magic" Johnson, Michael Jordan, Larry Bird, Charles Barkley and Scottie Pippen. Together they proved unstoppable and won gold.

Michael Jordan in action as part of the star-studded American basketball team.

A baskeball signed by athletes on the USA men's team at the Games.

Victory lap

When Ethiopian runner Derartu Tulu won the 10,000 metres race, she became the first female black African to win an Olympic medal. The second-place silver medalist was South Africa's Elana Meyer, who was white. In a memorable Olympic moment, the two athletes joined hands and ran a victory lap together, bringing the crowd to their feet. It was a moment that symbolized the end of apartheid, a system in South Africa that separated black people from white people.

Derartu Tulu celebrates her victory in the 10,000 metres with Elana Meyer.

Gymnast Vitaly Scherbo's signed competitor number.

Unified Team winner

Vitaly Scherbo put on an amazing performance as a member of the Unified Team, which was made of up athletes from the countries that used to be part of the Soviet Union. He won six golds in the gymnastics competitions, including the individual rings, parallel bars, pommel horse and vault events.

THE STARS OF
SEOUL 1988

Multiple medal wins defined the standout stars of Seoul. In the pool Matt Biondi was in awe-inspiring form, while track and field star Carl Lewis repeated his 1984 Olympic success by scoring wins in two events.

🇺🇸 Matt Biondi

In Seoul, American swimmer Matt Biondi equalled fellow swimmer Mark Spitz's record of winning seven Olympic medals at one Games edition. He won gold in the 50 and 100 metres freestyle, as well as all three relay races. He also won silver in the 100 metres butterfly and bronze in the 200 metres freestyle event.

🇺🇸 Carl Lewis

American sprinter Carl Lewis won gold in the 100 metres and the long jump, and a silver in the 200 metres, adding to the four golds he won at the Games in Los Angeles four years earlier. He would go on to win two more Olympic golds in 1992 and one more in 1996.

THE STARS OF
BARCELONA 1992

The Games in Barcelona saw the emergence of stars who would go on to shine for years to come. Both Deng Yaping and Aleksandr Popov were young athletes at their first Olympic Games and became multiple medal winners.

Deng Yaping

Standing just 1.49 metres tall, Den Yaping proved that height wasn't necessary to become a giant in table tennis. Yaping won two table tennis gold medals in Barcelona, first with her partner Qiao Hong in the women's doubles and then against her in the women's singles event! Yaping would win the same events in the 1996 Olympic Games in Atlanta.

Aleksandr Popov

Aleksandr Popov's coach, Gennady Touretsky, convinced the swimmer to switch from backstroke to freestyle and showed him videos of the great American freestyle swimmer Matt Biondi to help him train. In 1992, Popov beat Biondi in both the 50 and 100 metres freestyle events. He went on to repeat his double win in Atlanta in 1996, and also won a silver in the 100 metres freestyle in Sydney in 2000.

1996
ATLANTA

A century after the first modern Olympic Games took place in Athens, the city of Atlanta warmly welcomed the world to celebrate the Games' 100th anniversary in true Southern style.

GAMES STATS

Opening date:
19 July 1996

Closing date:
4 August 1996

Country of host city:
United States (USA)

Nations: 197

Events: 271

Emotional moments

The 1996 Games got off to a joyful start with an Opening Ceremony that featured the history of the US South and the origins of the Olympic Games. These Games will be remembered for emotional moments too. Boxer Muhammed Ali, who then had Parkinson's disease, struggled to lift the Olympic torch and light the cauldron at the Opening Ceremony. Later, on 27 July, a bomb blast in the city's Olympic Centennial Park killed one person and injured 110 others.

The Atlanta Olympic torch design was inspired by ancient torches made from a cluster of reeds bound by twine.

The Atlanta Olympic Stadium was the scene of an emotive Opening Ceremony.

FAST **FACT**
Atlanta's colourful mascot was Izzy, which featured in its own cartoon.

Programme additions

Many new Olympic events appeared in Atlanta 1996. Beach volleyball, lightweight rowing and mountain biking were new events for both men and women. There was also a new women's cycling road time trial event. In team sports, women's football, softball and a team rhythmic gymnastics event were added.

Ecuador's Jefferson Perez in full stride in the 20 km race walk event.

Cadel Evans of Australia in action in the women's mountain bike race.

Medal firsts

Several athletes in Atlanta made history in the track and field events. Jefferson Perez won the 20 kilometres race walk event and came home with the first ever Olympic medal won by a competitor from Ecuador. Men's 800 metres runner Vebjorn Rodal set an Olympic record on his way to becoming the first Norwegian athlete to win an Olympic athletics medal.

Speeding success

Sprinter Donovan Bailey of Canada proved unstoppable as he raced to gold in the men's 100 metres event and, in doing so, set a new world record of 9.84 seconds. Bailey also won gold as a member of the Canadian men's 4 x 100 metres men's relay team.

Donovan Bailey celebrates a stunning victory as part of Canada's 4 x 100 metres men's relay team.

2000
SYDNEY

A new millennium had arrived and for the second time in Olympic history, the Games were held Down Under. The 2000 Olympic Games were a celebration of local culture and sporting heroes.

Designed in three parts, the Sydney Olympic torch represents earth, sun and water.

GAMES STATS

Opening date:
5 September 2000

Closing date:
1 October 2000

Country of host city:
Australia (AUS)

Nations: 199, plus 4 individual athletes

Events: 300

Australian history

Australia's culture and history shone through in these Games, from the route of the torch relay to the choice of mascots. The Olympic flame was taken to the sacred Aboriginal landmark Uluru and even for an underwater swim along the Great Barrier Reef! The official poster used colours that evoked the Australian landscape while a trio of Olympic mascots were inspired by animals native to Australia.

The Games emblem on the official poster was inspired by a boomerang and the Sydney Opera House.

GAMES OF THE XXVII OLYMPIAD   JEUX DE LA XXVIIe OLYMPIADE   Sydney 2000

Plush versions of the three mascots from the 2004 Olympic Games.

FAST FACT

Blink and you might have missed Judo champion Ryoko Tamura winning gold. She won her final bout in just 36 seconds!

Local hero

Sydney-born swimmer Ian Thorpe was nicknamed the "Thorpedo" (which sounds like "torpedo") because of his speed in the swimming pool. Thorpe won gold as part of the Australian men's 4 x 100 metres and 4 x 200 metres freestyle relay teams, and another gold in the 400 metres freestyle in a world-record time. He also won silver in the 200 metres freestyle.

Australia's Ian Thorpe in action in his home city.

The moment Australian athlete Cathy Freeman lit the Olympic cauldron was shown on TV screens around the world.

Female legends

At the Sydney Opening Ceremony, Australian sporting heroes Betty Cuthbert, Raelene Boyle, Dawn Fraser, Shirley Strickland, Shane Gould and Debbie Flintoff-King had the special honour of carrying the Olympic flame into the Olympic Stadium. They passed it to sprinting gold-medal hopeful Cathy Freeman, who represented a new generation of female sporting talent.

New events

The Olympic programme in Sydney featured many new competitions, particularly for women. Female athletes could now compete in water polo, modern pentathlon and weightlifting. In diving, new platform and springboard synchronised events for both men and women appeared. And for the first time, taekwondo and the triathlon were Olympic sports.

This protective helmet was worn by women's taekwondo gold medalist Jae-Eun Jung of South Korea.

THE STARS OF
ATLANTA 1996

Two of the leading lights at the 1996 Games delivered astounding performances. It wasn't the first Games for either Michael Johnson or Naim Suleymanoglu, but it would be among their most memorable.

Michael Johnson

American sprinter Michael Johnson arrived in Atlanta ready to win (after food poisoning had hindered his performances in 1992). Competing in the 200 metres event, he set a world record of 19.32 seconds to win gold, and clocked one of the fastest times ever to win the 400 metres. He would go on to win two more golds in Sydney in 2000.

Naim Suleymanoglu

Nicknamed "The Pocket Hercules" because of his short height of 1.47 metres, Naim Suleymanoglu could lift three times his own body weight when he was just 16 years old! Suleymanoglu won three weightlifting gold medals in three consecutive Olympic Games - at Seoul in 1988, Barcelona in 1992 and finally Atlanta in 1996.

THE STARS OF
SYDNEY 2000

With 199 nations taking part at the Olympic Games in Sydney, athletes from across the globe – and not just Australia – brought their best performances and made Olympic history Down Under.

 Cathy Freeman

From the moment Cathy Freeman lit the Olympic cauldron, she became one of the crowd favourites of the 2000 Games. She is an indigenous Australian, which means she descends from the first people to settle in Australia. There were big expectations for Freeman in Sydney, and she didn't disappoint. Freeman won gold in the 400 metres and became the first indigenous Australian to win an individual gold medal.

Steven Redgrave

In 2000 the British rower won his fifth gold medal in his fifth successive Olympic Games. His Games victory came in the coxless fours event, making him the most successful male oarsman in Olympic history. His final success is even more impressive because, just one year before, Redgrave had announced that he was suffering from diabetes and needed treatment with insulin.

2004
ATHENS

Designed by Andreas Varotsos, the Athens Olympic torch resembles an olive leaf.

In 2004, the people of Athens and Greece welcomed the Olympic Games home once again – 3,000 years after the first ancient Olympic Games were held at Ancient Olympia and 108 years after the first modern Olympic Games took place in Athens.

GAMES STATS

Opening date:
13 August 2004

Closing date:
29 August 2004

Country of host city:
Greece (GRE)

Nations: 201

Events: 301

Track triumphs

Great Britain's Kelly Holmes became the first woman to win the 800 metres and 1,500 metres double at one Olympic Games. Men's 110 metres hurdles champion Liu Xiang became the first athlete representing China to win Olympic gold in a track and field event.

Kelly Holmes on her way to winning gold in the women's 1,500 metres event.

A return to roots

The ancient Panathenaic Stadium staged the archery competitions and provided the finish line for the marathon. Shot put competitions were held in the stadium at Olympia – the site of the ancient Olympic Games.

Wrestling first

The 2004 Olympic Games saw the introduction of a variety of sports and events that until then had not been a part of the ancient Olympic Games or even the modern Games. Most notably, this included four freestyle wrestling events for female athletes.

Russia's Lorisa Oorzhak takes on Brigitte Wagner of Germany in the women's freestyle 48kg wrestling event.

The 2004 medals (gold shown here) feature a figure of Nike and the Panathenaic Stadium – a venue for the 1896 and 2004 Games.

British rowers Steve Williams, James Cracknell, Ed Coode and Matthew Pinsent celebrate their win in the men's coxless four final.

Water conquerers

In the pool, Jenny Thompson won her 12th Olympic relay medal as part of the US women's 4 x 100 metres medley team. Meanwhile, Great Britain's Matthew Pinsent (lead rower above) won his fourth successive gold in rowing, this time in the coxless four event but without his former partner Steven Redgrave.

2008
BEIJING

The Olympic Games held in the Chinese capital city of Beijing in 2008 was a celebration that spotlighted the country's traditions and culture as well as Beijing's modernity. Organizers wanted to bring the world together with the slogan "One World, One Dream".

A plush version of one of the five FUWAs chosen as Beijing's mascots.

GAME STATS

Opening date:
8 August 2008

Closing date:
24 August 2008

Country of host city:
People's Republic of China (CHN)

Nations: 204

Events: 302

Bird's Nest

One of the first stars of the 2008 Games was Beijing's newly built National Stadium. The design of the building was unique, with its curved steel frame made up of interconnecting sections, which made the exterior of the stadium look like twigs in a nest. As a result, the National Stadium became more commonly known as the Bird's Nest.

The Opening Ceremony saw a fireworks display light up the National Stadium in Beijing.

FAST
FACT

The number 8 is very lucky in China, so the Opening Ceremony started at 8pm on 8/8/2008. It proved lucky for American swimmer Michael Phelps, too – he won eight gold medals in Beijing!

The Beijing torch was made of lightweight aluminium and burned environmentally friendly fuel.

ATHLETICS

Women's 4x100m Relay

The use of different coloured jade made each Olympic medal unique.

Headline heroes

Some athletes made the headlines thanks to their great stories of triumph. Competing in his ninth Olympic Games, Canadian Ian Miller won his first Olympic medal in the equestrian team jumping event. He was the 2008 Games' oldest medalist at 61 years old. Meanwhile China's women's rowing team became national heroes after unexpectedly winning gold in the quadruple sculls event.

61-year-old Ian Millar proved that age was just a number in the equestrian events.

On the courts

In Beijing, top tennis professional Rafael Nadal achieved his dream of becoming an Olympic champion in the men's singles event. In the women's singles, there was a clean sweep as Russian players took all three podium spots. Meanwhile, sisters Serena and Venus Williams of the USA won the women's doubles and Switzerland's Roger Federer and Stan Wawrinka teamed up to win gold in the men's doubles.

Usain Bolt's running shirt and race number for his 200-metre sprint to gold.

Roger Federer and Stan Wawrinka in action in the men's doubles event in tennis.

Sprinting sensation

Usain Bolt made winning look easy as he raced to his first Olympic medal in world record time in Beijing. By the end of the Games, he had won a total of three gold medals, in the 100 metres, 200 metres and 4 x 100 metres relay. Each time, he celebrated with his trademark archer's pose.

THE STARS OF
ATHENS 2004

People around the world tuned in to watch the 2004 Games, in which athletes competed in 301 different events. In particular, swimmer Michael Phelps' performances saw records tumble. On the track, Morocco's Hicham El Guerrouj made up for past disappointments by winning double gold.

🇺🇸 Michael Phelps

Swimmer Michael Phelps made Olympic history when he set a Games record for a swimmer of eight medals, six gold and two bronze. He followed his Athens performance by claiming eight golds at Beijing 2008, four golds and two silvers at London 2012, and at Rio 2016 he won five more golds and a silver. He is the only swimmer in history to break five individual world records in one World Championship.

🇲🇦 Hicham El Guerrouj

Moroccan runner Hicham El Guerrouj was the favourite to win the 1,500 metres at his first Games in 1996, but he fell and finished last. In 2000, he finished second. His fortunes changed in 2004, when he won gold in both the 1,500 and 5,000 metres. It was the first time in 80 years that an athlete had achieved this double.

THE STARS OF
BEIJING 2008

Dreams came true in Beijing, when athletes who had already proved themselves in previous Olympic Games won even more medals and set new records.

Jingjing Guo

China's Jingjing Guo lived up to her nickname, the "Princess of Diving", in 2008. She had already won medals in three previous Olympic Games editions, and in Beijing she did it again. She teamed up with Minxia Wu to win the 3 metres synchronized springboard event. Then she won a second gold in the individual springboard. Her total of six Olympic medals was the highest ever for a female diver.

Peter and Pavol Hochschorner

Twins Peter and Pavol of Slovakia, who are known jointly as "Pepa", worked together in the water to achieve what no paddlers had done before them. They won three gold medals in the men's C-2 canoe slalom over three Olympic Games, between 2000 and 2008. Canoeing clearly runs in the family, as both their parents and their sister also competed in the sport.

LONDON

London hosted the Games of the XXX Olympiad, which saw the celebration return to the capital for a third time. The planning of the 2012 Games honoured London's Olympic past and focused on urban regeneration as part of its enduring legacy.

The 8,000 perforated circles in the London torch symbolized the achievements of each of the London 2012 torchbearers.

GAMES STATS

Opening date:
27 July 2012

Closing date:
12 August 2012

Country of host city:
Great Britain (GBR)

Nations: 204 and 4 individual athletes

Events: 302

Green legacy

The organisers transformed an area of East London into a leafy Olympic Park that would be left as a legacy for the people after the celebrations. Spread over a huge area of 560 acres, the park featured natural greenery and waterways mixed with a variety of sports venues. The Olympic Village was located within walking distance of all the venues in the Park.

Spectators enjoying the atmosphere in the green spaces of Olympic Park.

FAST FACT

A new cycling event called the omnium first appeared at London 2012. The event tested cyclists in six disciplines of track cycling, contested over two days.

Wenlock's design was inspired by a taxi cab light, a camera lens and the Olympic stadium roofline.

Women's boxing

The introduction of women's Olympic boxing in 2012 meant that women competed in all sports for the first time at the Games. The first medals were awarded to competitors in the flyweight division, for women weighing 48 to 51 kilograms. Great Britain's Nicola Adams won the gold medal. Cancan Ren, Mary Kom and Marlen Esparza also won medals.

Nicola Adams in action against Cancan Ren of China during the women's 48-51kg boxing final.

Buckingham Palace was one of London's iconic sights on the Olympic marathon route.

A royal view

The route of the Olympic marathon offered members of the British royal family the opportunity to watch Ugandan Stephen Kiprotich on his way to the finish line on the Mall, just outside Buckingham Palace. The race route passed other famous London landmarks too, including the Tower of London, the Houses of Parliament and Trafalgar Square.

Triathlon photo finish

The women's event In the triathlon provided a dramatic result. Switzerland's Nicola Spirig won gold and Lisa Nordén of Sweden took the silver as they finished only 15 centimetres apart. In the men's event, British brothers Alistair and Jonny Brownlee delighted local fans, as Alistair won gold and Jonny finished third to take the bronze medal.

Nicola Spirig crosses the finish line first, just ahead of Lisa Nordén.

2016
RIO

The torch's triangular shape represents the Olympic values. The mascot Vinicius (below) is named after the poet of Bossa Nova.

The Olympic Games travelled to South America for the first time in 2016. The Games offered a carnival of colour, music and culture mixed with notable sporting firsts and triumphs.

GAMES STATS

Opening date:
5 August 2016

Closing date:
21 August 2016

Country of host city:
Brazil (BRA)

Nations: 205, 1 refugee Olympic team and 9 Independent Olympic Athletes

Events: 302

Brazilian flavour

The Games in Rio de Janeiro celebrated both Brazilian culture and the coming together of the world's athletes. The Games' official poster, torch, tickets and medals reflected the vibrant look of the country. The colours of Brazil's nature and wildlife, as well as the curves of Rio's Sugarloaf Mountain, inspired their design.

Shootout drama

In Rio's Maracanã Stadium, Brazil played Germany in the final of the men's football tournament. The action-packed game came down to a nail-biting penalty shootout. It was kick for kick until Germany missed the fifth spot-kick and Brazil scored, giving Brazil's team its first ever Olympic football gold.

The official poster features the emblem of the Games.

The triumphant Brazilian men's football team delight the home crowd.

88

Rugby history

For the first time since 1924 rugby returned to the Games, which also saw the introduction of a women's rugby event. The Australian team took home the first gold Olympic medal in the women's competition. Meanwhile, Fiji's team went undefeated in the men's event, scoring a 43-7 victory in the final to take home the first-ever Olympic medal won by athletes representing the country.

Australia's team triumphed over Great Britain's team in the women's rugby final.

A record haul

Michael Phelps won six more golds in Rio to take his overall Olympic medal tally to an incredible record-setting 28. One gold that he did not add to his total was in the men's 100 metres butterfly, as Singapore's Joseph Schooling showed the world that Phelps wasn't invincible. Phelps, South Africa's Chad Le Clos and Hungary's László Cseh ended up in a three-way tie for silver.

FAST **FACT**

After 112 years, golf made its Olympic return in Rio de Janeiro. It was played at a newly built Olympic golf course in the Barra region of the city.

Recycled metals were partially used to make the Olympic medals sustainable.

The winner and the three silver medalists of the 100 metres butterfly pose to give the media a rare photo opportunity.

XXXI Olimpíada Rio 2016

THE STARS OF
LONDON 2012

Two multi-medal-winning Olympians stole the show at the Games in London. They each competed in five Olympic Games and won medals, making them the most successful competitors in the history of their sports.

🇮🇹 Valentina Vezzali

A member of Italy's female fencing team, Valentina Vezzali produced an outstanding display of foil work at the Games in London. She earned the nickname the "Cobra" because of her speed and accuracy. Over the course of five Olympic Games (from 1996 to 2012), she won six gold medals, one silver and two bronze.

🇬🇧 Ben Ainslie

This tough and tactical sailor won gold in the Finn class sailing event at the Games in London, and not for the first time. He won the same title in 2004 and 2008. Ainslie switched to the Finn from the laser class event after competing at the 1996 and 2000 Games, where he won silver and then gold. Surprisingly, Ainslie named all his boats Rita!

THE STARS OF
RIO 2016

Both Usain Bolt and Kaori Icho came to the Olympic Games for a fourth time in 2016, and both left with even more gold medals! In doing so they each confirmed their legacies as Olympic legends of their sports.

Usain Bolt

His massive stride and lightning-bolt pose made Usain Bolt a star, but it was his positive, never-give-up attitude that made him a sprinting legend. After placing fifth in the 200 metres event in Athens in 2004, Bolt went on to win eight gold medals in the next three Olympic Games. At Rio, he won the 100 metres, 200 metres and 4 x 100 metres relay in what was his last time competing at the Olympic Games.

Kaori Icho

Both women's wrestling and Japan's Kaori Icho made their fourth appearance at the Games in 2016. Icho was undefeated between 2003 and 2015, but she had a lot to prove in Rio following an unexpected loss in January 2016 that had ended an epic winning streak. But she was back on form in Rio, becoming the first-ever female athlete to win four consecutive individual Olympic titles.

2020
TOKYO

Fifty-six years after the city last hosted the Games in 1964, Tokyo will again welcome the world in 2020 with plans designed to make it a celebration of Japan's new generation and emerging technologies.

The 2020 torch features a traditional Japanese Sakura-mon cherry blossom shape.

GAMES STATS

Opening date:
24 July 2020

Closing date:
9 August 2020

Country of host city:
Tokyo (JPN)

Events: 339

Counting down

The handover of the Olympic flag from the mayor of Rio de Janeiro to the mayor of Tokyo was just one of the special moments in the countdown to the 2020 Olympic Games. Since Tokyo was elected as Olympic host in September 2013 there have been a number of events to celebrate the "days to go" to the Games in 2020. These events have all built up anticipation for the celebration and have also inspired the people of Japan throughout the planning stages.

The first ever coloured coin issued by the Japanese mint celebrates the Olympic flag handover ceremony.

FAST FACT

Robots will join the 80,000 human volunteers at the 2020 Games! They will greet athletes and guests at Olympic venues and offer their assistance to spectators in wheelchairs.

The "2020 Days to Go" celebration held in Tokyo.

2020 Days to Go!!

Youth participation

Japan's young people have had lots of opportunities to take part in planning for the 2020 Games. Young Olympic hopefuls could take part in the "2020 Young Athletes" project and learn about Olympic values. Meanwhile school children have planted flowers to be used at the Olympic venues and have also helped to choose the Olympic mascot, Miraitowa. The mascot's name combines the Japanese words "mirai" (which means future in English) and "towa" (which means eternity).

The Tokyo 2020 mascot, Miraitowa, features the blue and white patterns of the official 2020 Games emblem.

Recycled metal

The people of Japan can claim that they helped to make the Tokyo 2020 Olympic medals. This is because they had the opportunity to donate old electronic devices such as mobile phones, digital cameras and laptops. The gold, silver and bronze metals collected from the devices were then processed to be used in the Olympic medals.

Even Olympic athletes donated their electronic devices so that the metals in them could be used to make the 2020 medals.

Olympic Agenda 2020

Thanks to the Olympic Agenda 2020 recommendations, the Tokyo Organizing Committee was able to add extra sports to the 2020 programme. Among the sports chosen were those that are popular locally and internationally, plus appeal to young people. This means that Tokyo 2020 will include an additional 18 events across five sports, which are baseball/softball, karate, skateboarding, sport climbing and surfing.

Sport climbing events will be one of the new competitions included for Tokyo 2020.

INDEX

1948 LONDON

Engraved with the Olympic rings, this standard torch was made of stainless steel.

Two Olympic Games editions had been cancelled in 1940 and 1944 because of the Second World War. In 1948, the Olympics returned once again to London to bring athletes of the world together.

Olympic effort

In 1948 Great Britain was still recovering from the Second World War, so there was a shortage of places to stay, food and equipment. Olympic organizers had to be creative with what they already had. They used existing sports venues instead of building new ones. They arranged for athletes to stay in army camps, schools and hotels. And many countries gave gifts of food – Denmark donated 160,000 eggs!

OLYMPIC GAMES

29 JULY 1948 14 AUGUST
LONDON

The official poster of the Games of the XIV Olympiad shows Big Ben and the Houses of Parliament.

A starters' pistol and a camera used at the 1948 Games.

GAMES STATS

Opening date:
29 July 1948

Closing date:
14 August 1948

Country of host city:
Great Britain (GBR)

Nations: 59

Events: 136

New technology

The world had changed since the last Olympic celebration and there were new technologies that could help both organizers and athletes in sporting events. Starting blocks were used for the first time, to help runners have faster starts. The starters' pistol, which signals the start of a race, was linked to an electronic race timer. And a camera could be used to decide on the winner of a close finish.

THE STARS OF
BERLIN 1936

Amid Germany's political backdrop, it was African-American sprinter and long jumper Jesse Owens who emerged as the most popular athlete in Berlin. Meanwhile, the 1,500 metre race produced another hero in New Zealand's John Lovelock.

 ## Jesse Owens

Jesse Owens was a huge star of Berlin 1936. He won gold medals in the 100 metres, 200 metres, the long jump and the 4 x 100 metres relay. Born in Alabama, he was the youngest of 10 children and was christened James Cleveland Owens. A schoolteacher misheard him when he said his name was "J. C. Owens" and he was known as Jesse ever after.

John Lovelock

John Lovelock became New Zealand's first Olympic champion in 1936, in the 1,500 metres race. In a fiercely fought final, Lovelock beat American Glenn Cunningham to the gold medal. Both competitors broke the world record, and the three competitors who finished behind them broke the Olympic record!